ZAPIRO

My Big Fat Gupta Wedding

Cartoons from *Mail & Guardian*, *Sunday Times* and *The Times*

Acknowledgements: Thanks to my editors at the Mail & Guardian *(Nic Dawes, Chris Roper), at the* Sunday Times *(Ray Hartley, Phylicia Oppelt) and at* The Times *(Stephen Haw) and their production staff; writers at my three newspapers and at* Independent Newspapers, City Press, *the* Daily Maverick *and* SAPA *for a few choice phrases used in my captions and for the title of this book; my website, ePublications and rights Manager Richard Hainebach; my assistant Eleanora Bresler; Bridget Impey, Russell Martin and all at Jacana; Claudine Willatt-Bate; Nomalizo Ndlazi; and my family: Karina, Tevya and Nina.*

10 Orange Street
Sunnyside
Auckland Park 2092
South Africa
(+27 11) 628 3200
www.jacana.co.za

in association with

ISBN 978-1-4314-0844-3

Cover design by Jonathan Shapiro

Page layout by Claudine Willatt-Bate
Printed by Ultra Litho (Pty) Ltd, Johannesburg
Job no. 002102

See a complete list of Jacana titles at www.jacana.co.za

See Zapiro's list and archive at www.zapiro.com

For Karina, again and always

ZAPIRO annuals

The Madiba Years (1996)

The Hole Truth (1997)

End of Part One (1998)

Call Mr Delivery (1999)

The Devil Made Me Do It! (2000)

The ANC Went in 4x4 (2001)

Bushwhacked (2002)

Dr Do-Little and the African Potato (2003)

Long Walk to Free Time (2004)

Is There a Spin Doctor In the House? (2005)

Da Zuma Code (2006)

Take Two Veg and Call Me In the Morning (2007)

Pirates of Polokwane (2008)

Don't Mess With the President's Head (2009)

Do You Know Who I Am?! (2010)

The Last Sushi (2011)

But Will It Stand Up In Court? (2012)

Other books

The Mandela Files (2008)

VuvuzelaNation (2013)

4 October 2012

Just weeks after police killed 34 striking miners at Marikana, the ANC looks ahead to its year-end conference as more miners vent anger and transport strikers torch trucks

5 October 2012

7 October 2012

The Constitutional Court rules that Menzi Simelane, appointed by the president to be National Director of Public Prosecutions, is dishonest and unsuitable

9 October 2012

Has the state really spent over R200 million upgrading President Jacob Zuma's private home at Nkandla? They won't tell us. Public Protector Thuli Madonsela is looking into it.

14 October 2012

Illusionist's electrifying stunt at Pier 54 in New York

18 October 2012 Narrow the wage gap by denying yourselves salary increases and bonuses, he tells top execs

21 October 2012

Her fierce independence has earned her ANC attacks in parliament and widespread respect elsewhere

18 October 2012

At the six-month-old paper funded by the Zuma-linked Gupta brothers

16 October 2012

Austrian daredevil jumps from space. A damning report finally nails former hero Lance Armstrong as the world's biggest doping cheat.

25 October 2012

They want to hike tariffs by 16% per year for five years.
Promises to cut costs exclude their 10% bonuses on already fat salaries.

28 October 2012

Four years after he sued over a cartoon showing him abusing the justice system, the president drops the case on the eve of going to court

30 October 2012

Out of court, presidential spokesman Mac Maharaj recycles the accusations and claims Zuma dropped charges to promote free speech

4 November 2012

Mad anniversary

1 November 2012 It's two months till the ANC's conference at Mangaung and pundits say his re-election is sewn up

CYRIL RAMAPHOSA in

The Rake's Progress

M&G 25-10-12 ZAPIRO ©

after Hogarth (1733) and Searle (1955)

EMERGENCE

Defies apartheid regime as heroic mining unionist. Lands coveted spot holding Madiba's release speech.

SUCCESS

Heads transition talks with NP counterpart, Roelf Meyer.

TRIUMPH

Delivers Constitution. Annointed by Madiba.

TEMPTATION

Volunteers for cadre deployment billionnaires' programme. Excels. Develops gravy addiction.

DEGRADATION

Bids R18 mill. for buffalo. Private e-mails to fellow-bosses during miners' strike reveal he speaks baasskap fluently.

DOWNFALL

Mangaung, Dec. 2012: accepts ANC deputy presidency.

RUIN

2019: becomes President.

25 October 2012

He's back in politics and tipped to be Zuma's party deputy. Now an e-mail he wrote before the Marikana shootings paints him as a mine boss urging tough action against the strikers.

23 October 2012

Ahead of the US presidential election

AS AMERICAN AS...

©ZAPIRO THE TIMES 5-11-12

5 November 2012

It's perplexing to the outside world that run-up polls have flaky Republican Mitt Romney running level

8 November 2012 The 'four more years' photo of Barack and Michelle breaks social media records

8 November 2012

Dodging DA leader Helen Zille's questions on Zuma's home, spin doctor Maharaj slams her 'colonial language'. The SABC's head of news promptly issues a terminology ban.

15 November 2012 SA Communist Party general secretary Blade Nzimande backs the call for a new law

15 November 2012

22 November 2012

Pressed over public funds splurged on his private home, he told Parliament he had a bond. Mac says proof will be furnished, but not to media. Yeah, sure.

'Dinner time at Nkandla', a fish and chip advert featuring the prez and his wives, is banned by the SABC. Meanwhile, some Cabinet ministers have been doing some splurging of their own.

29 November 2012

22 November 2012 The US vetoes a UN resolution condemning Israel's rocket strike that killed 19 civilians in Gaza

20 November 2012

Starting in De Doorns, a bitter strike for the minimum wage to increase from R71 to R150 a day has spread across the Western Cape

27 November 2012

At the Democratic Alliance's congress, re-elected leader Helen Zille outlines ambitions to woo disaffected ANC voters and get 30% of the national vote in the 2014 election

29 November 2012

One month to go. The party is fractious but the top spot is secure, whether or not current deputy Kgalema Motlanthe contests it.

2 December 2012

Sucking up to China, government last year prevented the Dalai Lama from attending Archbishop Tutu's 80th birthday party

4 December 2012

A week in which we lose Madiba's former right-hand man
Jakes Gerwel, 66, and former Chief Justice Arthur Chaskalson, 81

6 December 2012

Now we know why journos Sthembiso Msomi, Sam Mkokeli and Andrew England couldn't be on Sakina Kamwendo's 'Road to Mangaung' show

6 December 2012

Motlanthe, the ANC's thoughtful deputy, may contest for party presidency.
Ramaphosa, the ANC's billionaire, is the next talent lined up to deputise for mediocrity.

9 December 2012

R7 million in payments, umpteen benefactors. An auditor's report, buried when his corruption case was dropped in 2009, is exposed in the media

13 December 2012

13 December 2012 Doomsday hype: December 21 is the last day on the ancient Mayan long-count calendar

16 December 2012 Big weekend for the ANC and for the SA premiere of *The Hobbit: An Unexpected Journey*

18 December 2012 A twist to secretary-general Gwede Mantashe's report on disunity and disruptive forces

20 December 2012

23 December 2012

Broadly welcomed in his new party position,
Ramaphosa will have to wind up his business interests

15 January 2013 Careful, don't outshine the boss – rather call him an action man (*giggle*) at a party rally

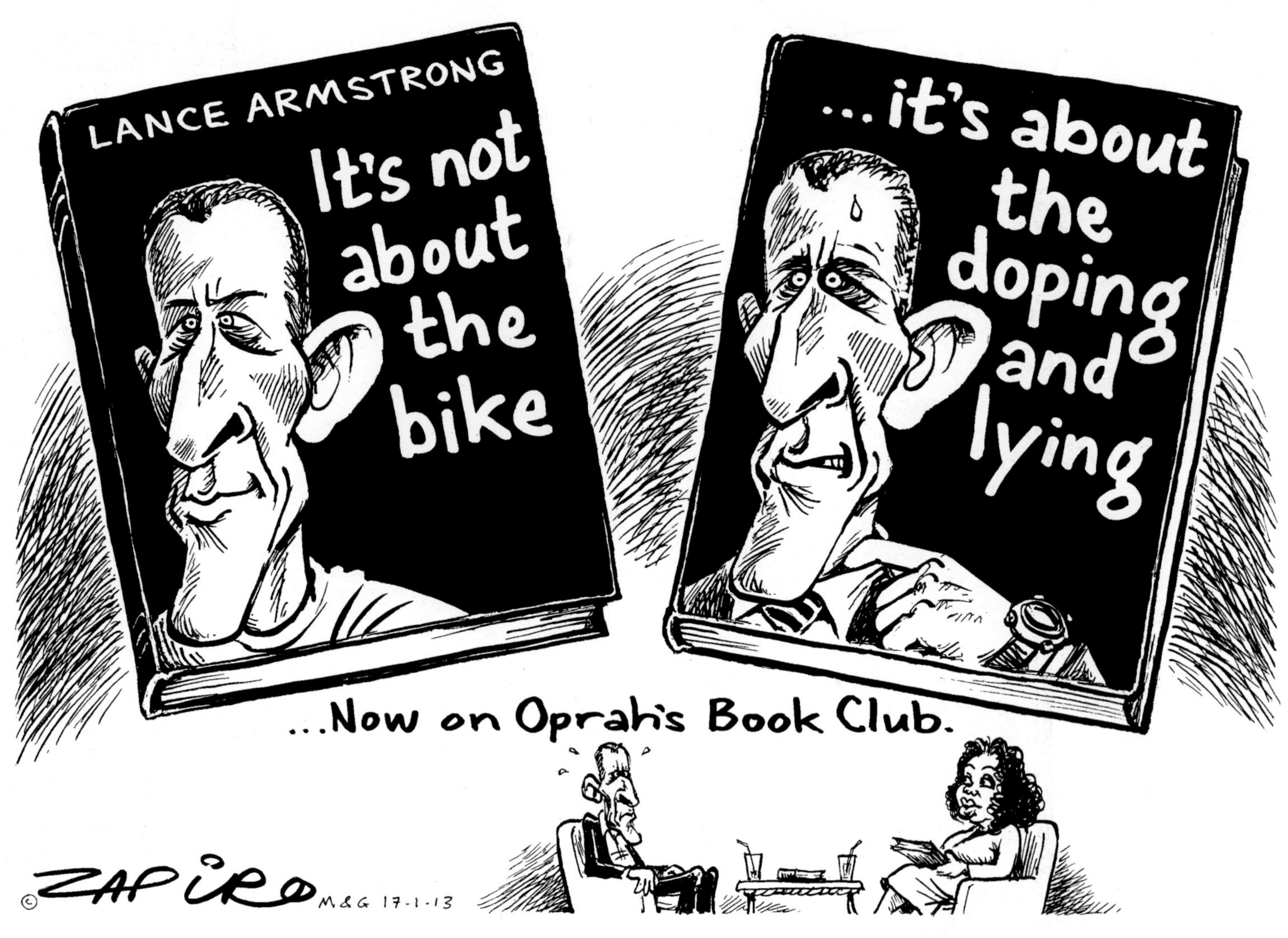

17 January 2013 Coming clean, sort of. A stage-managed TV confessional is safer than testifying to the authorities.

22 January 2013

The Cape is still in turmoil as the nation hosts the African Cup of Nations.
The home team looks better under the new coach but still couldn't score against lowly Cape Verde.

24 January 2013

In a video clip shown at the Marikana Commission of Inquiry, the policemen who gunned down 34 miners are praised by National Police Commissioner Riah Phiyega for their responsible actions

24 January 2013

SA's growth forecast is downgraded as he arrives at the annual forum

29 January 2013

R206 million spent on 'security upgrades', no public spending on the private home itself, is what Public Works Minister Thulas Nxesi says is in his secret report. At least the ANC believes him.

31 January 2013

It's that smell of cover-up again. Respected attorney Mokgale Moabi quits Judge Willie Seriti's Commission of Inquiry, saying the judge has a 'second agenda'.

27 January 2013

Zuma's sugar-daddies, the Guptas, also give to the ANC and promote it in their paper. Tit-for-tat, R25 million has been siphoned out of state-owned enterprises to fund *New Age* business breakfasts.

31 January 2013

They're acting on orders from the Department of Public Enterprises.
The profitable breakfasts are live on SABC as a freebie to the paper.

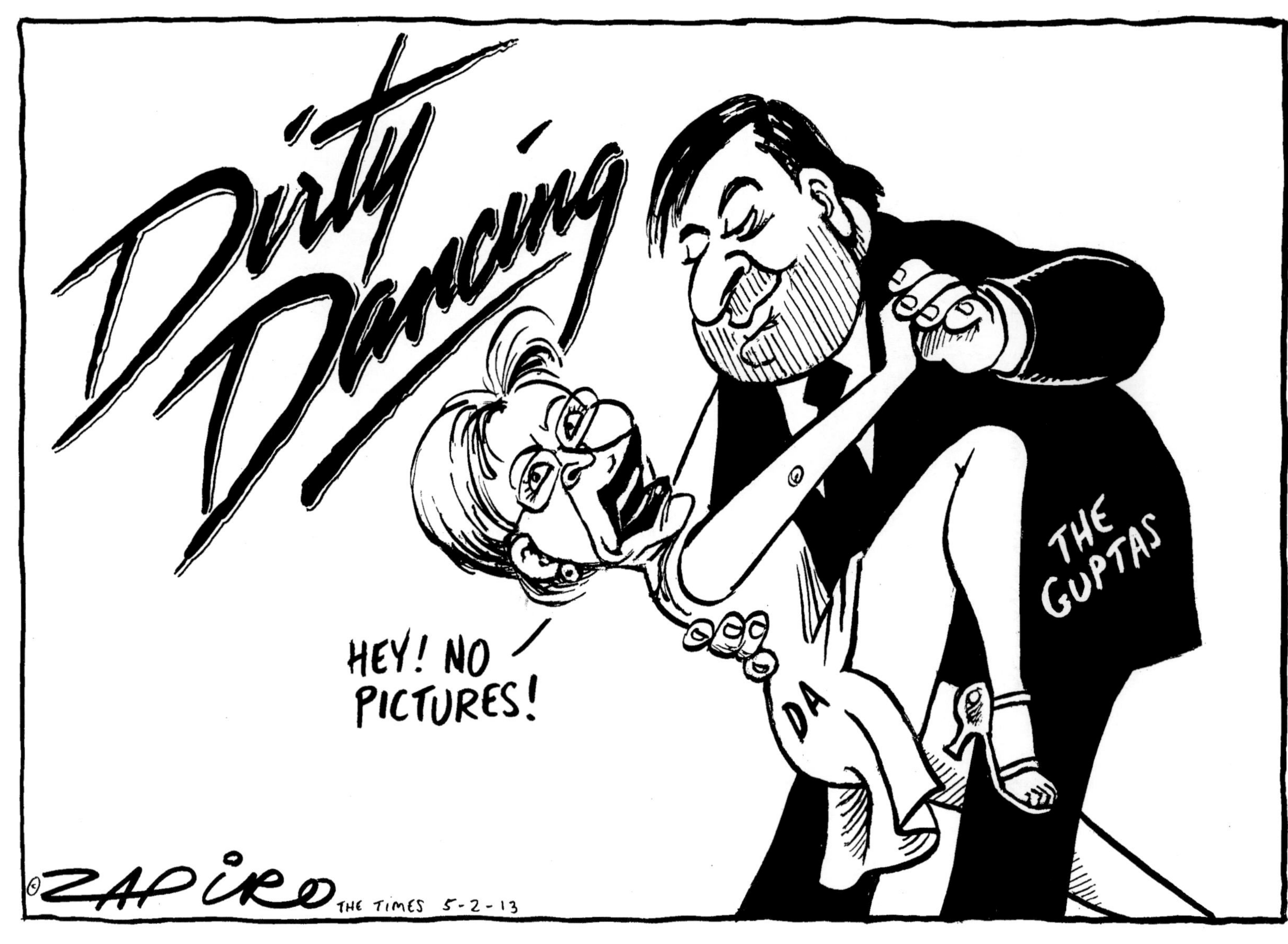

5 February 2013

Hitting back after Zille shuns a *New Age* breakfast, the paper publishes a letter from her thanking the Guptas for a R200 000 cheque to the DA that she accepted at the Gupta residence in 2009

10 February 2013 The parent company of *The New Age* will soon launch a new 24-hour TV channel

12 February 2013 The Zille–*New Age* spat prompts renewed calls for disclosure of party funding to be compulsory

7 February 2013

Broad hints of soon-to-be-launched party. Dr Mamphela Ramphele, a respected businesswoman, academic and former activist, is untested as a politician.

7 February 2013

As the ANC grumbles that the FNB's scripted 'You Can Help' campaign uses children to portray government negatively, a particularly brutal crime makes headlines

14 February 2013

Annual address falls on Valentine's Day

Valentine's day story: Star athlete Oscar Pistorius faces murder charges.
He denies knowing it was his girlfriend, model Reeva Steenkamp,
who was in the bathroom when he fired four shots through the door.

17 February 2013

At Oscar's bail hearing, the detective in charge admits he didn't wear protective shoe coverings and also missed a cellphone and a spent bullet in the toilet (and all this before we hear that he himself faces seven charges of attempted murder)

21 February 2013

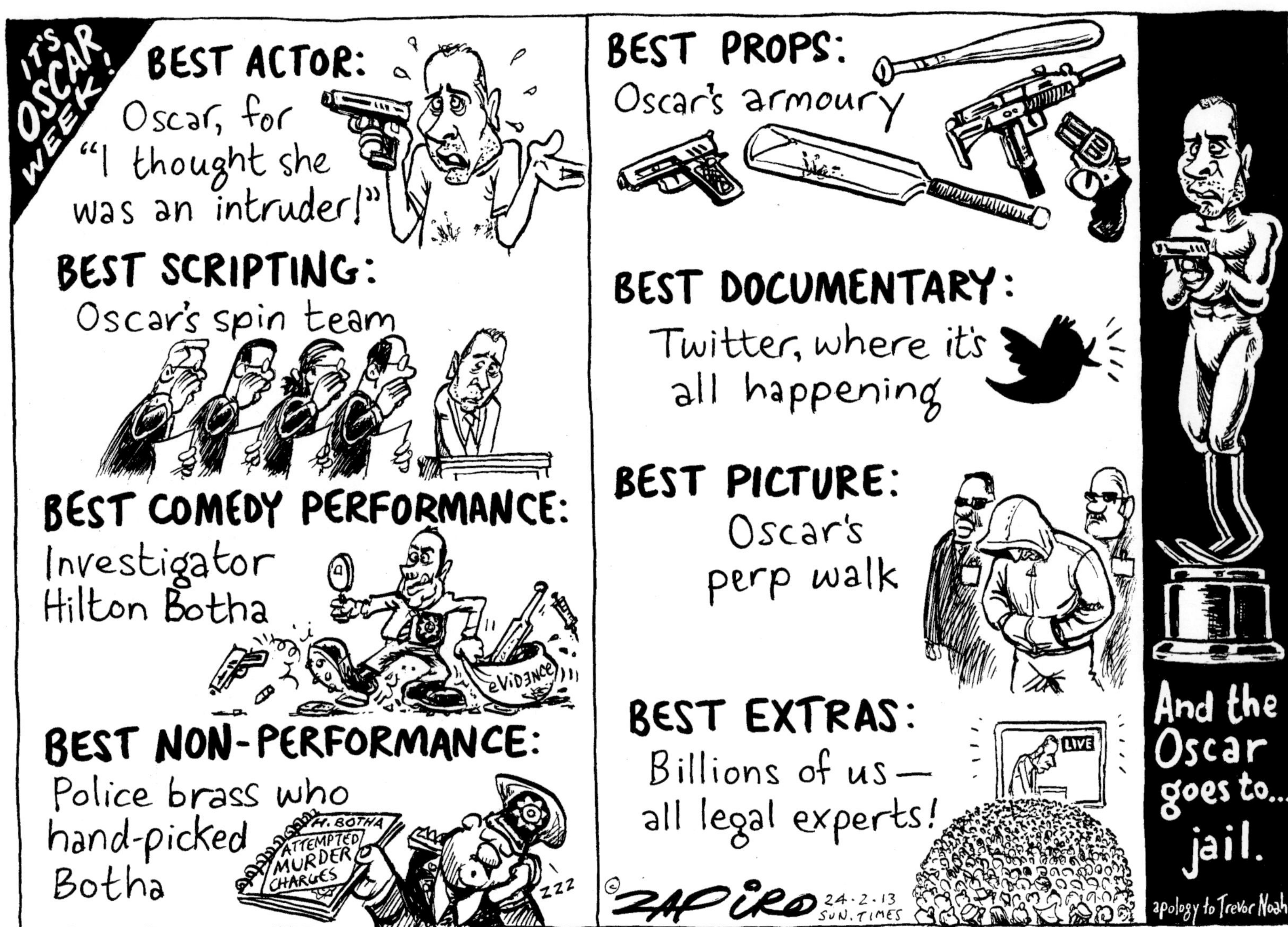

24 February 2013

Botha gets replaced, Oscar gets bail, the hearing gets global coverage

26 February 2013

The Oscar for best documentary goes to *Searching for Sugar Man*, the story of the forgotten muso tracked down in Detroit by two SA fans

19 February 2013

After her announcement speech, we know her new party's name
and that she's very cross about how we've been let down since 1994

28 February 2013

Donkey, goat and water buffalo have been found in two-thirds of burgers and sausages tested by researchers

7 March 2013

A video of police dragging taxi driver Mido Macia behind a van goes viral, as does news that he bled to death hours later after a savage police beating

5 March 2013

Eight cops are charged with murder. The call for top brass to resign is taken as seriously as the thought that absent Minister Mthethwa should interrupt his honeymoon.

7 March 2013

Cosatu general secretary Zwelinzima Vavi, the ANC's main critic within its alliance with unions, is accused of corruption over the purchase of new Cosatu premises

7 March 2013

Cancer claims Venezuela's charismatic president

10 March 2013

Death at 57 of the apartheid killer cop who founded the Vlakplaas death farm and later blew the lid on atrocities after an internal fall-out

12 March 2013

If you thought International Criminal Court charges of crimes against humanity over Kenya's 2007 election violence might handicap Uhuru Kenyatta at the polls, think again

28 February 2013 The pressure gets to Benedict. He's the first pope to quit in 600 years.

14 March 2013

An Argentinian cardinal becomes Pope Francis, the first pope from outside Europe

17 March 2013

They're still in spin mode when a second dragging by cops is reported and there's news of a third (which turns out to be fatal)

20 March 2013

The Youth League's leadership, which backed Motlanthe's Mangaung bid to oust Zuma, is disbanded by the parent body

24 March 2013

Mass exodus of SABC board members due to meddling by the Minister of Communications, who is to be probed by Parliament for mismanagement

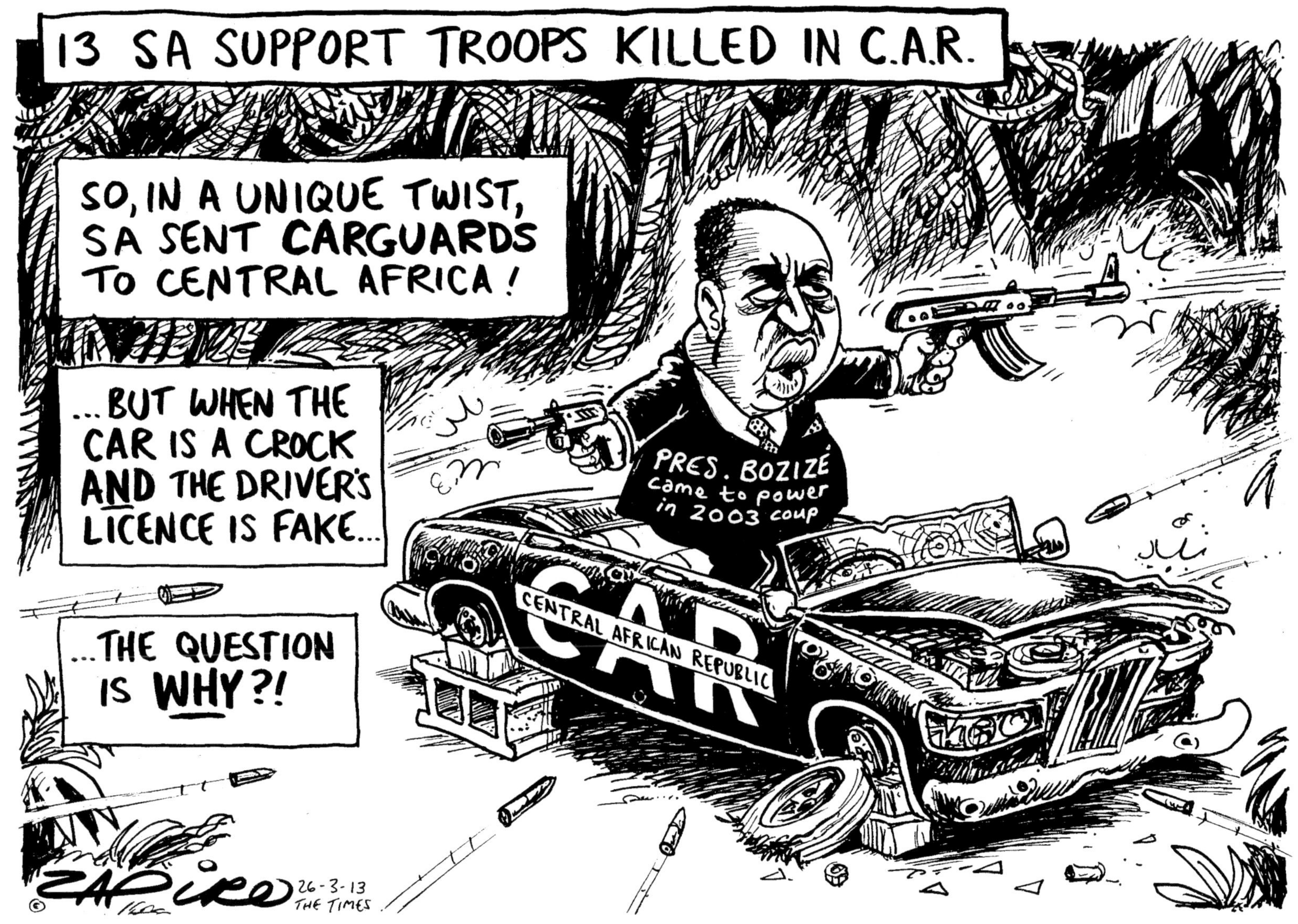

26 March 2013

As rebels topple the dodgy regime, our government scrambles to explain our troops' presence. The press smells shady business.

Sure enough, during the president's Durban hosting of the 5th Brics summit, the *Mail & Guardian* reveals that our troops were in the CAR to protect mining interests linked to ANC politicians

27 March 2013

4 April 2013

His condolences differ in tone from the ANC statement accusing the *M&G* of 'pissing on the graves of gallant fighters'

31 March 2013

3 April 2013 For the third time in recent months, Nelson Mandela is admitted to hospital with a recurring lung infection

4 April 2013

North Korea's Kim Jong-un is 'settling accounts with Washington' by declaring a state of war with South Korea

9 April 2013 Goodbye to the 'Iron Lady'

11 April 2013 With her boyfriend she's looted millions, as the parliamentary committee headed by Ben Turok finds out

14 April 2013

As he lies ill, this round of the trust fund war is daughters vs grandson

16 April 2013

Judicial Service Commission member Izak Smuts
has resigned in protest over the JSC's anti-intellectual approach

18 April 2013 The Reserve Bank transfers a R914 million loan to top up Zimbabwe's election budget

18 April 2013 Three dead, 180 injured in the two bomb blasts at the Boston Marathon finishing line

21 April 2013

Rebranding campaign with a touch of photo-opportunism

24 April 2013

Sentenced in absentia over the death in 2002 of a young leukaemia patient, Cape Town professor Cyril Karabus has been arrested while passing through the UAE. Eight months and two acquittals later, dubious legalities block his release.

25 April 2013

The corruption claim against Vavi looks like a purge attempt by Cosatu chairman Sdumo Dlamini and others who've been co-opted onto ANC structures

28 April 2013

The Protection of State Information Bill is passed in the National Assembly amid warnings of its impact on democracy

2 May 2013

Somehow a commercial jet flies from India to an SA military base with 200 guests who bypass customs and get a multi-departmental VIP welcome

2 May 2013 Influence-peddling so blatant that everyone's outraged, even the ANC

5 May 2013

The bride is Atul Gupta's niece, the lavish affair is in Sun City,
the blame is pinned on India's High Commissioner and two lowly officials
and the guest of honour is so embarrassed he won't attend

Q. What do these gates have in common?
NKANDLAGATE
C.A.R.GATE
GUPTAGATE
A. The Secrecy Bill – if it were already signed into law, you'd know nothing about any of them.
THE TIMES 7.5.13
ZAPIRO ©

7 May 2013

9 May 2013

Repeating his vow to shut down the military prison at Guantanamo Bay, President Obama blames Congress for blocking him

9 May 2013

Equal Education's solidarity visit to the Eastern Cape finds everything from windows and toilets to the whole school system broken

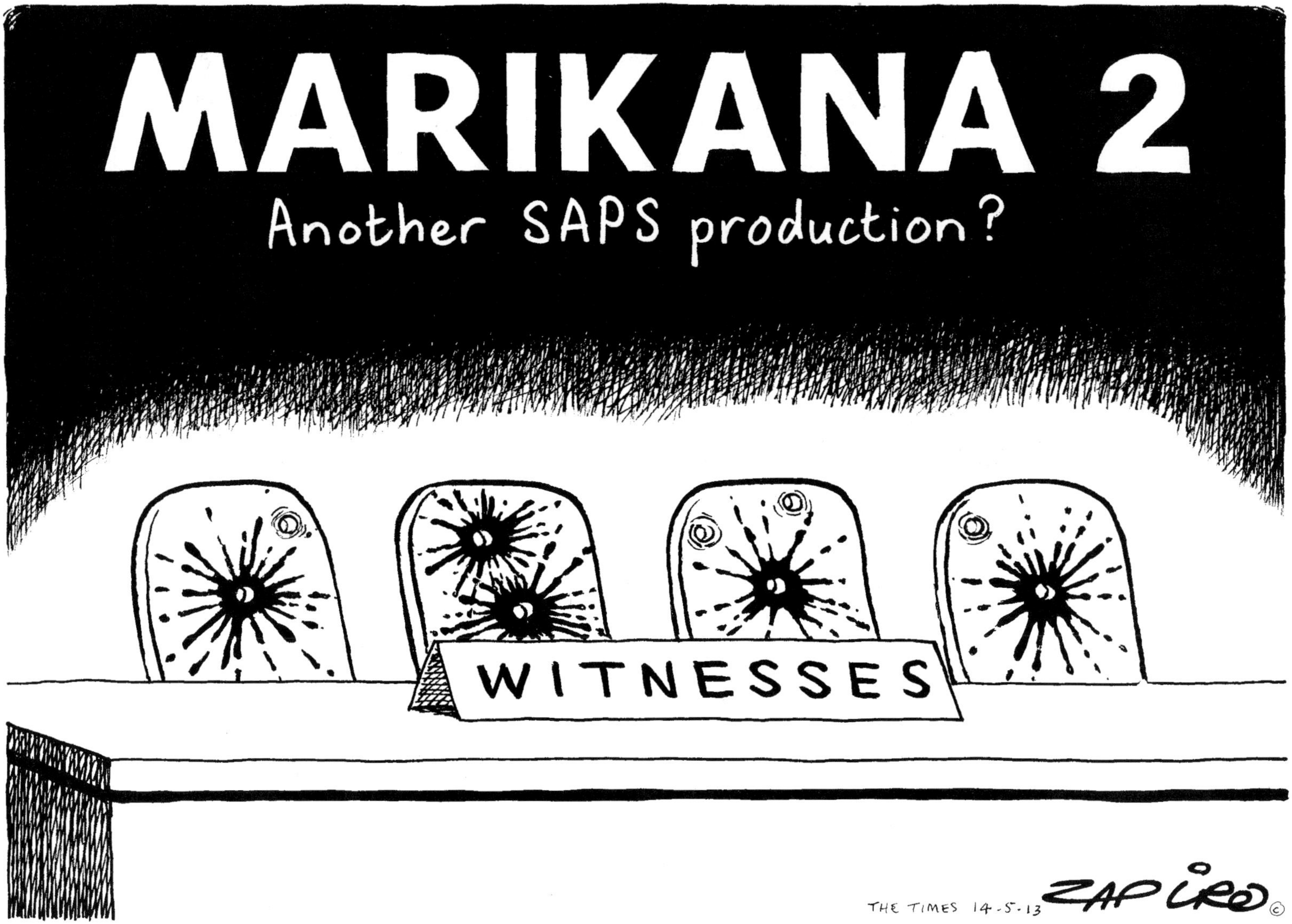
MARIKANA 2
Another SAPS production?
WITNESSES
THE TIMES 14-5-13
ZAPIRO ©

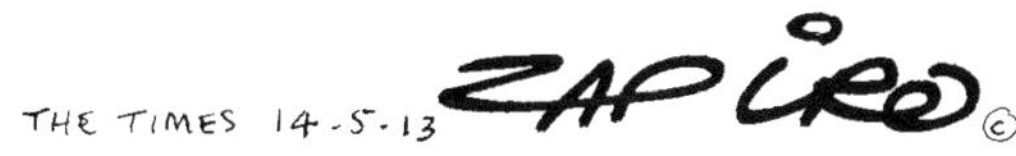

14 May 2013

Union organiser Steve Khulekile is the fourth potential witness to be gunned down before testifying at the Farlam Commission of Inquiry investigating the Marikana killings

19 May 2013

The Great Gatsby remake

©ZAPIRO M&G 16-5-13
WELCOME DR. KARABUS
HELD 9 MONTHS IN U.A.E.
... HOME AT LAST, SIR!
?
GUPTASTAN
G
OUR PRESIDENTS:
OUR PRIME MINISTER
RE-ENTRY →
GUPTASTANI CITIZENS
GUPTASTAN
G

16 May 2013

26 May 2013

No mention of high-level wrongdoing in Minister of Justice Jeff Radebe's report to parliament. One of the three official fall-guys is state protocol chief Bruce Koloane, who said he was 'under pressure from Number One'.

Obama will visit SA soon. Cape Town mayor Patricia de Lille plans to award him the Freedom of the City. Meanwhile she and her DA leader have been targeted by poo protesters demanding flush toilets.

6 June 2013

9 June 2013

There's talk of an Olympic bid

11 June 2013

Former CIA technician releases a mass of classified info to highlight US spying on citizens and the collusion of the major service providers

21 May 2013

Sudden loss of the well-loved radio and TV presenter with the signature sign-off

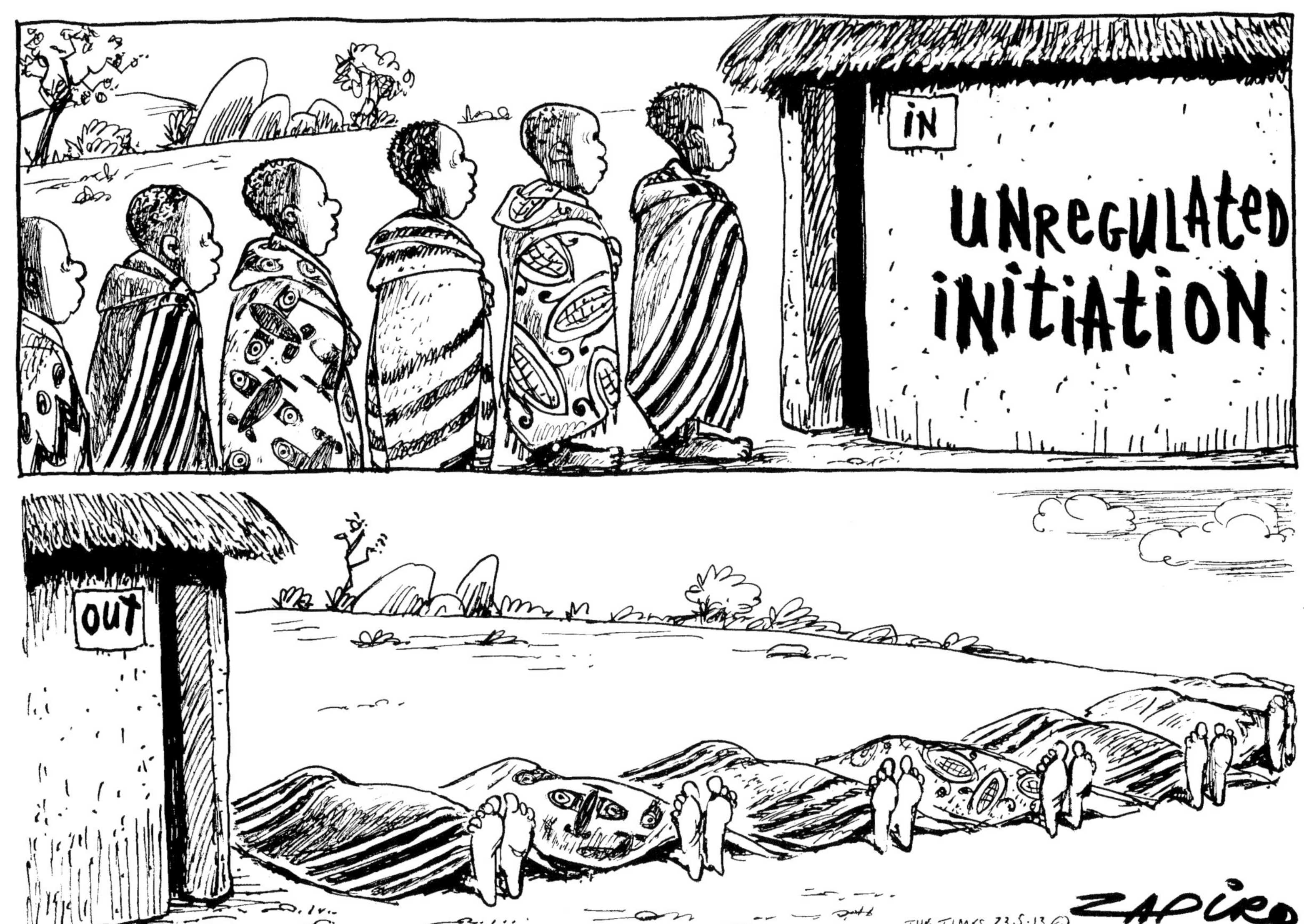

23 May 2013 Maltreatment and unsafe circumcisions have killed 33 young men in the first month of initiation season

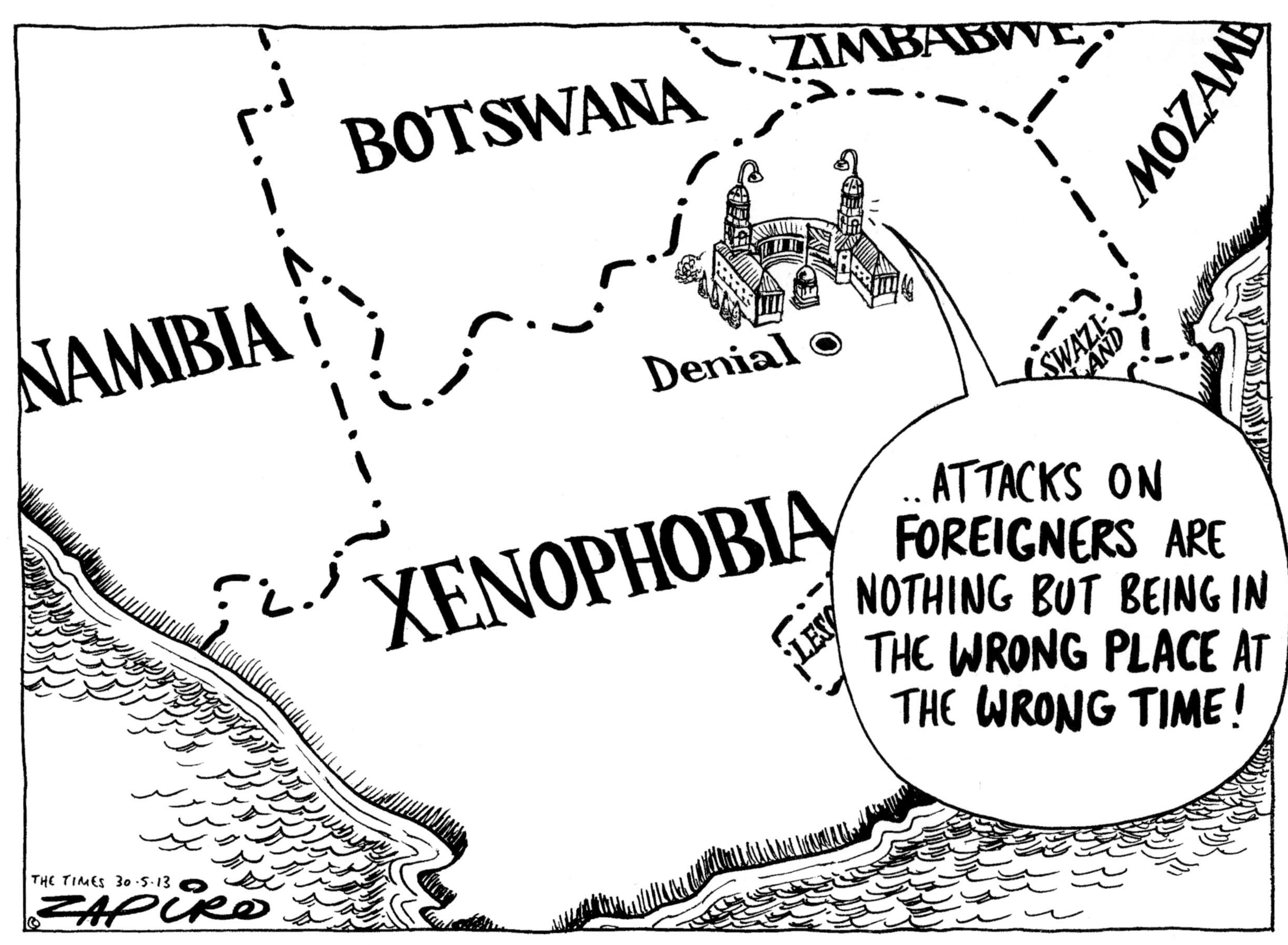

30 May 2013

Refusing to use the x-word, authorities blame common criminality for Gauteng's spate of attacks on shops owned by foreigners

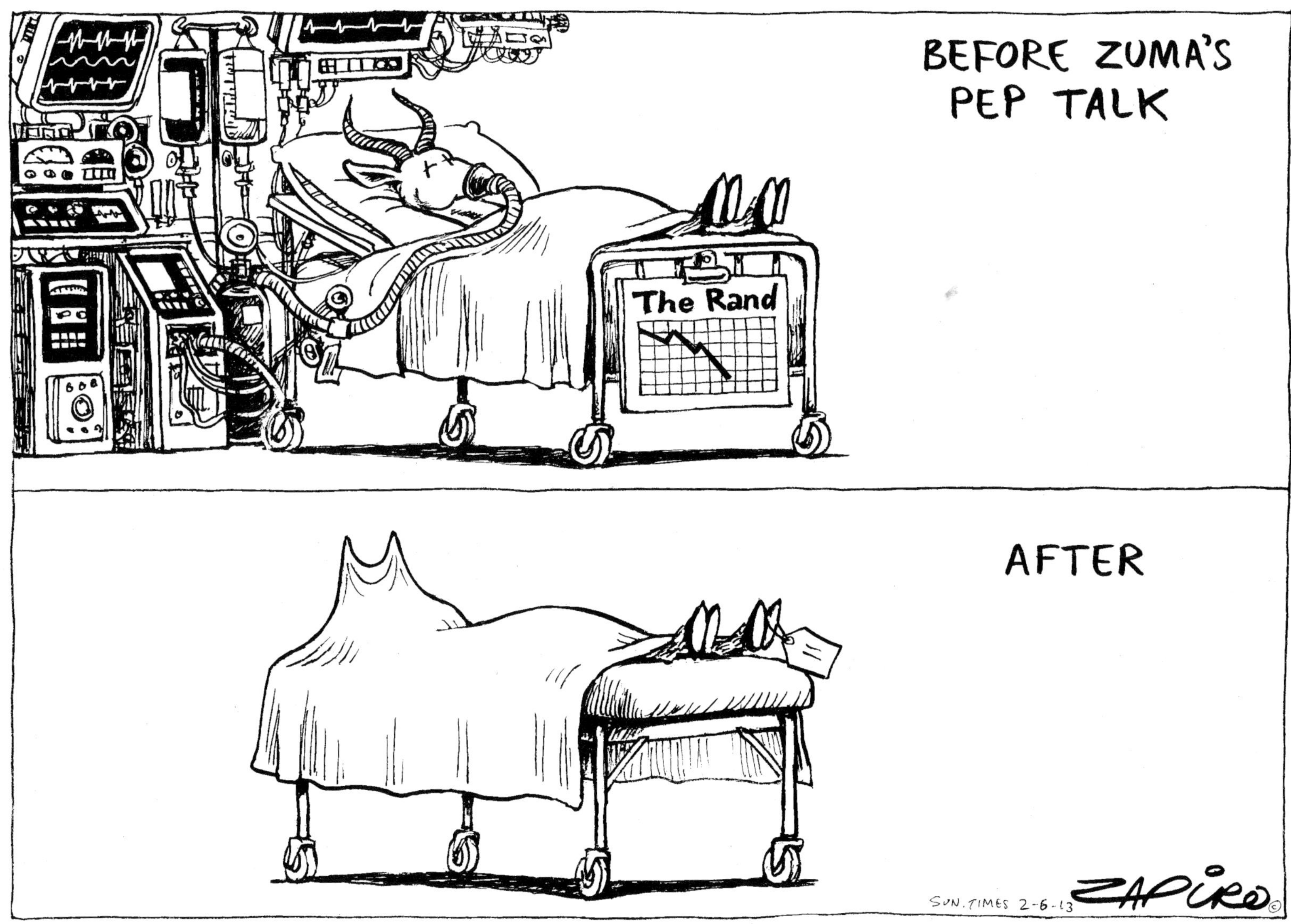

2 June 2013 His special briefing was aimed at halting the rand's free-fall through R10 to the dollar

4 June 2013

Mutual schmoozing on *People of the South*

30 May 2013

It's one blundered case after the next for the National Prosecuting Authority as all 15 trumped-up charges against prosecutor Glynnis Breytenbach are thrown out of court

13 June 2013

News goes global that his sixth recent hospitalisation is the most serious yet

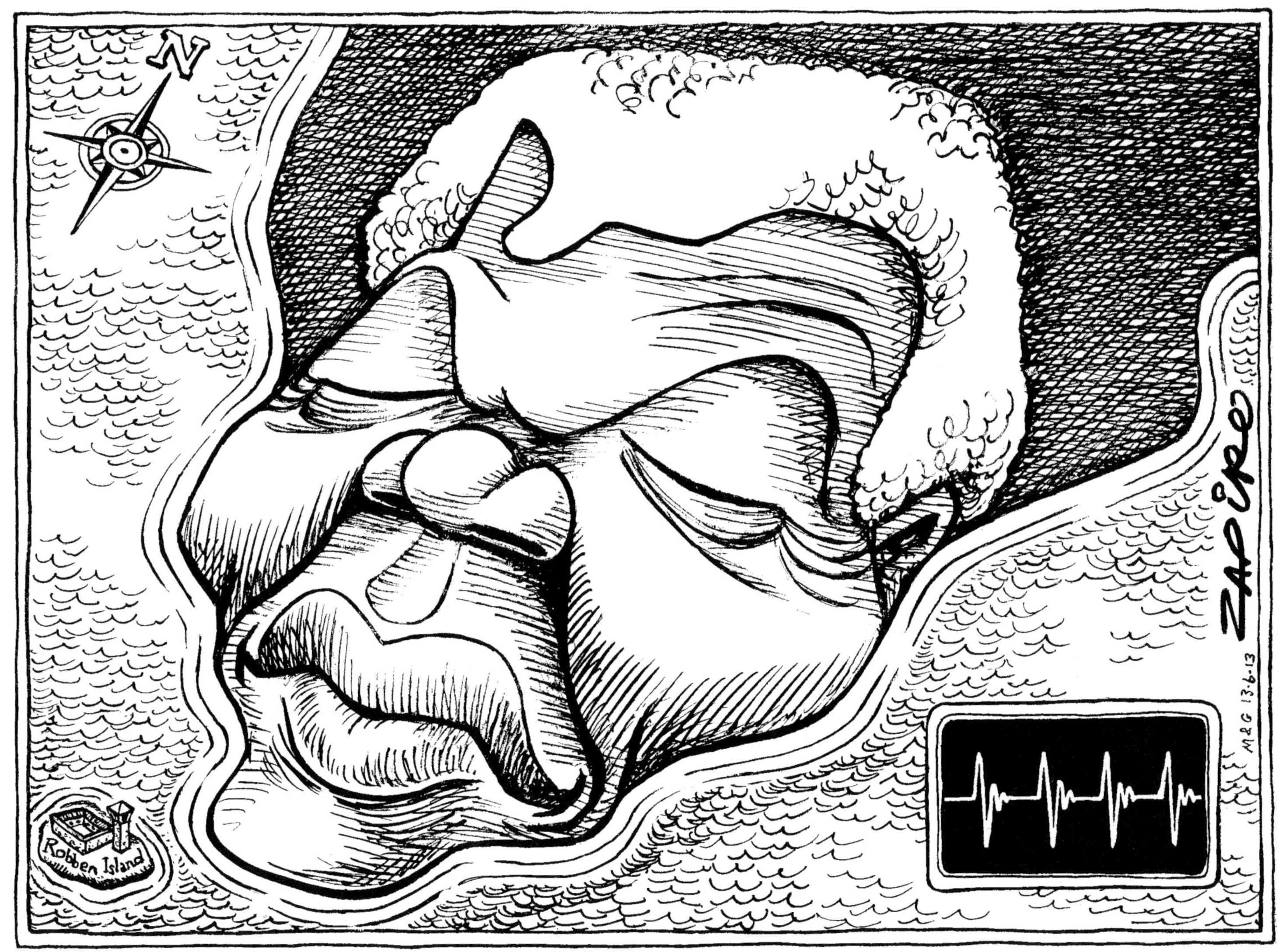

13 June 2013

16 June 2013

Relief as his condition improves a bit

18 June 2013

Expelled ANC Youth League leader Julius Malema, still facing money laundering charges, is busy launching the Economic Freedom Fighters party

20 June 2013

Centenary of the law that forced black people into reserves and ceded 87% of the land to the white minority

"Those who can, do.

Those who cannot, teach."

—GEORGE BERNARD SHAW

...Those who are just useless, become Minister of Education.

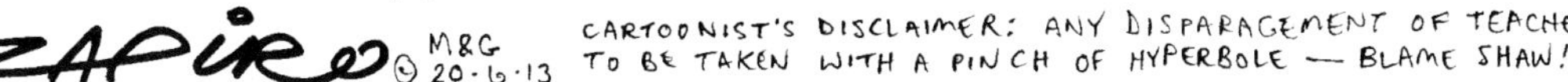

Pressured to publish the minimum education standards she's promised, Basic Education Minister Angie Motshekga calls Equal Education activists 'a group of white adults organising black children with half-truths'

20 June 2013

25 June 2013 Another scathing speech at the launch of the party with the funny name

27 June 2013

Touching down for his first visit to SA as US president

10 July 2013

Andy Murray's victory over world number one Novak Djokovic makes him the first British male in 77 years to win his country's premier event

11 July 2013

Cabinet reshuffle. Among the axed are the rotten Dina Pule and Human Settlements Minister Tokyo Sexwale, who backed Zuma's opponent at Mangaung.

16 July 2013

Survival of the loyalists

11 July 2013 Fifty years since the raid that led to the Rivonia Trial

14 July 2013

The daughters' faction goes to court to stop grandson Mandla from exhuming family remains – and that's just *this* week's headline

18 July 2013 His 95th birthday and the fourth international Mandela Day

18 July 2013

Details revealed of the SA 2010 World Cup stadium collusion
that distorted tenders, inflated profits and arranged losers' kickback fees

21 July 2013 Eastern Cape DA leader Athol Trollip has recruited the AbaThembu king

23 July 2013

At the Durban Film Festival, the screening of a new SA movie about a teacher's predatory involvement with a 16-year-old pupil is cancelled. It's been labelled 'child porn' and banned.

1 August 2013

Smackdown unbanning by their own appeals committee

25 July 2013

After Mugabe calls Zuma's adviser an 'idiotic street woman' for saying Zimbabwe isn't ready for credible elections, her boss disowns her comment

1 August 2013

'I'll go if I lose'. Fat chance. Independent monitors note the dubious electoral commission, the shambolic voters' roll and the usual harassment of opposition.

4 August 2013

Registration flaws have disenfranchised up to a million voters. Whatever.
It's thumbs up from Olusegun Obasanjo as head of the African Union's mission.

30 July 2013

Headline scandal. He admits to having an affair with the Cosatu official he recruited but denies her rape claim and accuses her of blackmail.

6 August 2013

Thousands of documents haven't been declassified in time, two researchers have quit in protest at Seriti's 'second agenda' and now a commissioner, Judge Legodi, quits too

7 August 2013

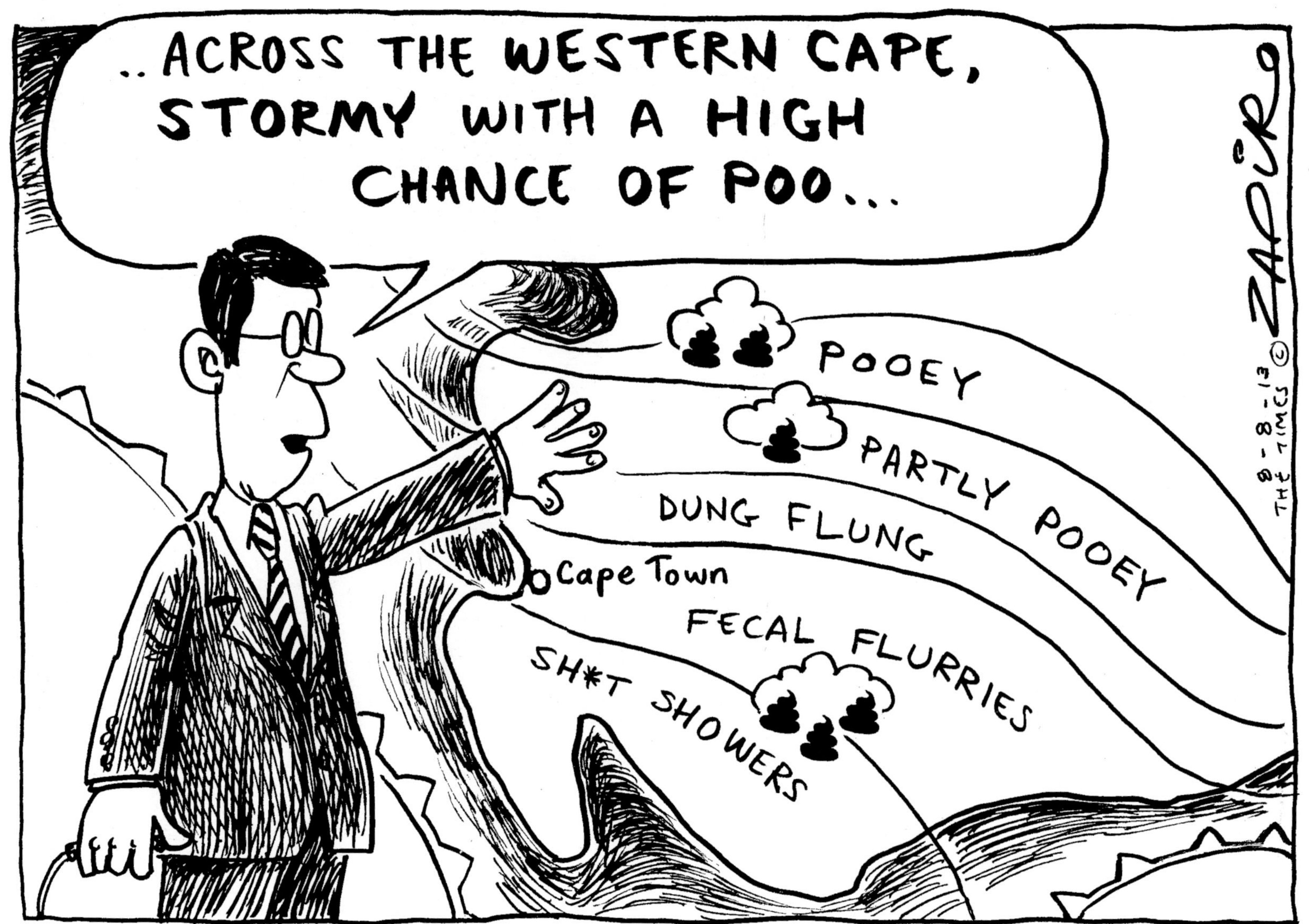

8 August 2013

This week's protests hit the provincial legislature steps,
Cape Town International Airport and various spots on the N2 Highway

13 August 2013 The legend takes the sprint double at the Moscow World Athletics Championship

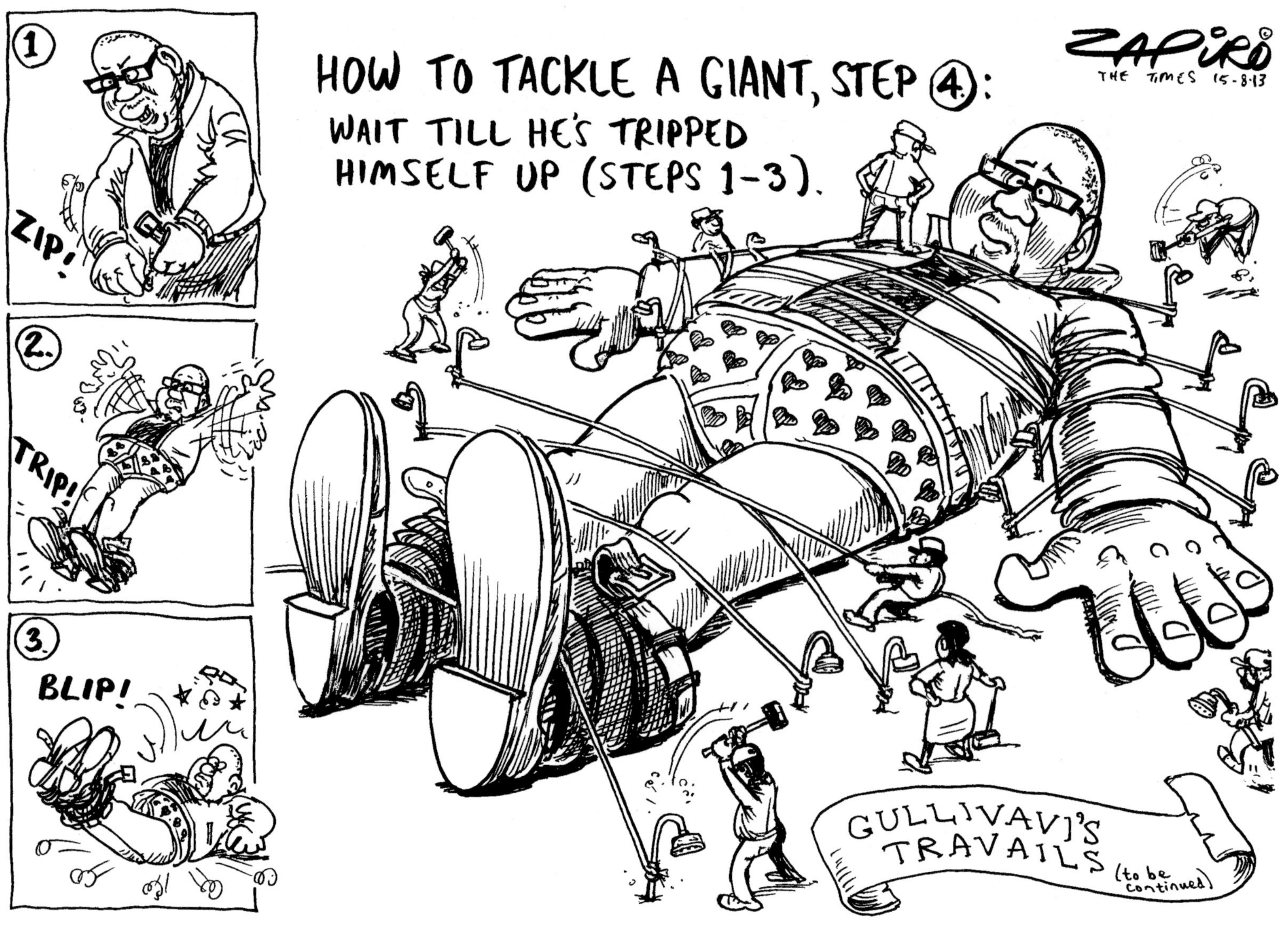

15 August 2013 His opponents are pushing to suspend him when Cosatu's central committee meets over his affair

15 August 2013

He is suspended

11 August 2013 They've nailed her on all charges and recommended the severest penalty Parliament can impose

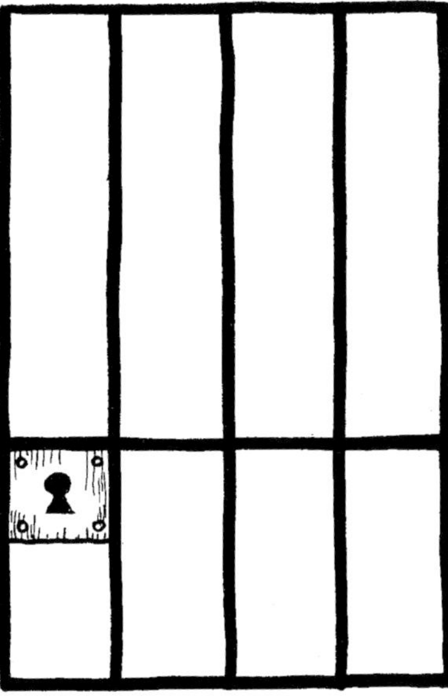

22 August 2013

She gets off with a parliamentary tongue-lashing and a two-week suspension from the House, and she'll forfeit just one month's salary

18 August 2013

21 August 2013

The High Court orders the NPA to hand the DA the spy tapes thought to show that corruption charges against him were dropped in 2009 as a political favour

24 August 2013 As expected, his lawyers will appeal the court's decision

22 August 2013 SABC's new 24-hour channel is soon followed by one that's even worse

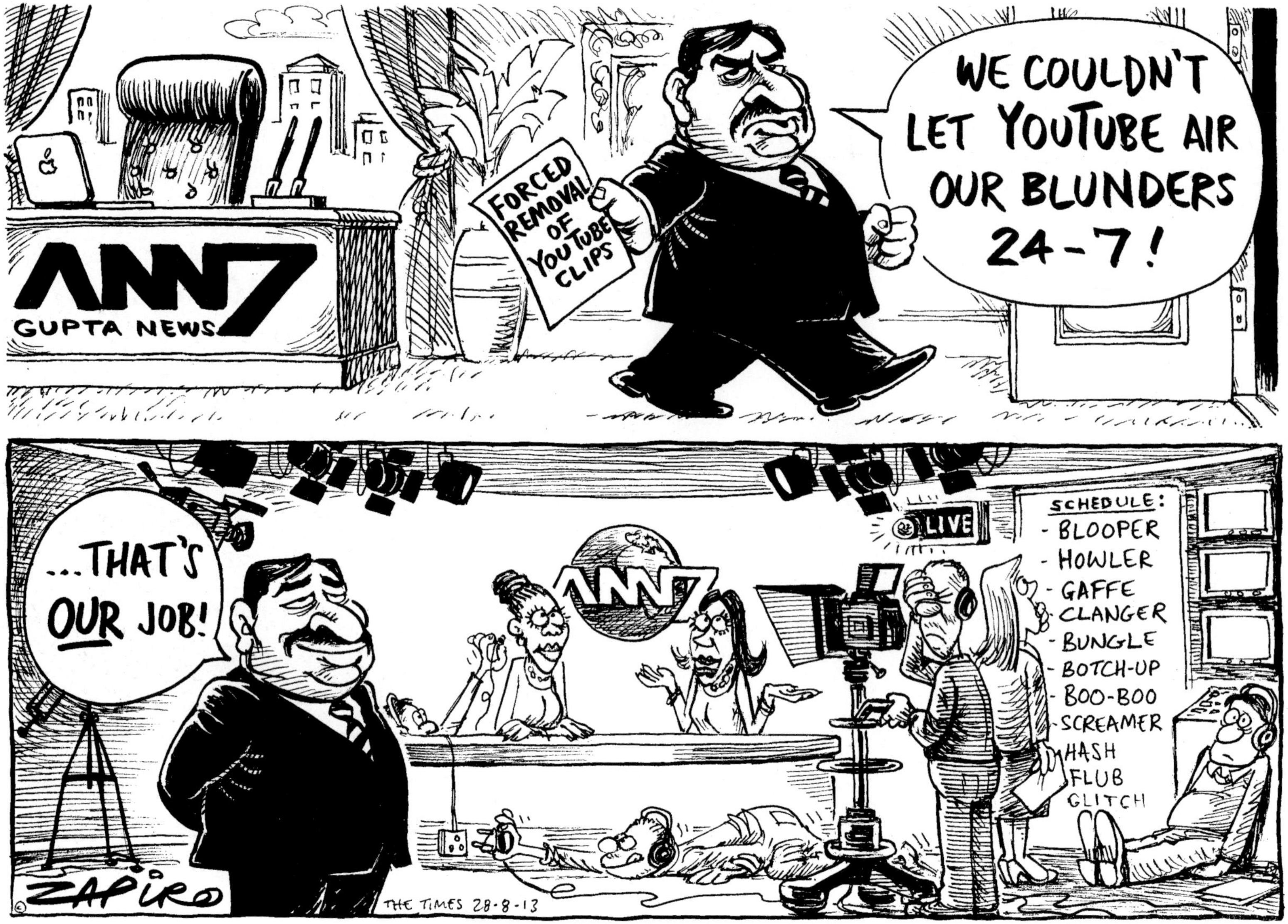

28 August 2013

29 August 2013

Public Protector's report fingers the Independent Electoral Commission's chairwoman. Winner of the hefty lease deal for the IEC's new premises is none other than her business partner and (ahem) boyfriend.

29 August 2013

Historic speech marked, 50 years on. Knowing a deadlocked UN won't punish Bashar al-Assad's regime for the recent poison gas attack on Syrian civilians, the US plans another 'coalition of the willing'.

1 September 2013

NEWS THIS WEEK..

4 September 2013

8 September 2013

While he's away, his legal team appeals the court decision ordering the handover of those pesky spy tapes

5 September 2013

5 September 2013

With Cosatu Zumafied under Sdumo Dlamini, metalworkers led by Numsa general secretary Irvin Jim try in court to get Vavi's suspension reversed

12 September 2013

Protest march over government's refusal to fund their representation (i.e. Advocate Dali Mpofu) at the Marikana Commission

12 September 2013

Under their famously matricless acting chief operating officer, they're unable to account for the huge amount in license payments that's come in and been spent

18 September 2013

Epic Springbok vs All Blacks clash in Auckland is spoiled when French ref Romain Poite yellow-cards powerhouse hooker Bismarck du Plessis for a perfectly good tackle and later red-cards him

19 September 2013

The salvage master who hoisted the *Costa Concordia* upright off Italy's coast in the biggest operation of its kind is a South African

24 September 2013

Annual release of crime figures. No one's buying her rosy picture, least of all the policing experts who show how raw data has been spun.

29 September 2013

UK-born 'White Widow' Samantha Lewthwaite, who holds an SA passport, is the suspected commander of Somalian Al-Shabab terrorists who've killed over 70 people in Kenya's 4-day mall siege

26 September 2013

Recent terror attacks have killed hundreds in Nigeria
and there are fears of co-ordination between jihadist groups

15 September 2013

Applauded for not signing

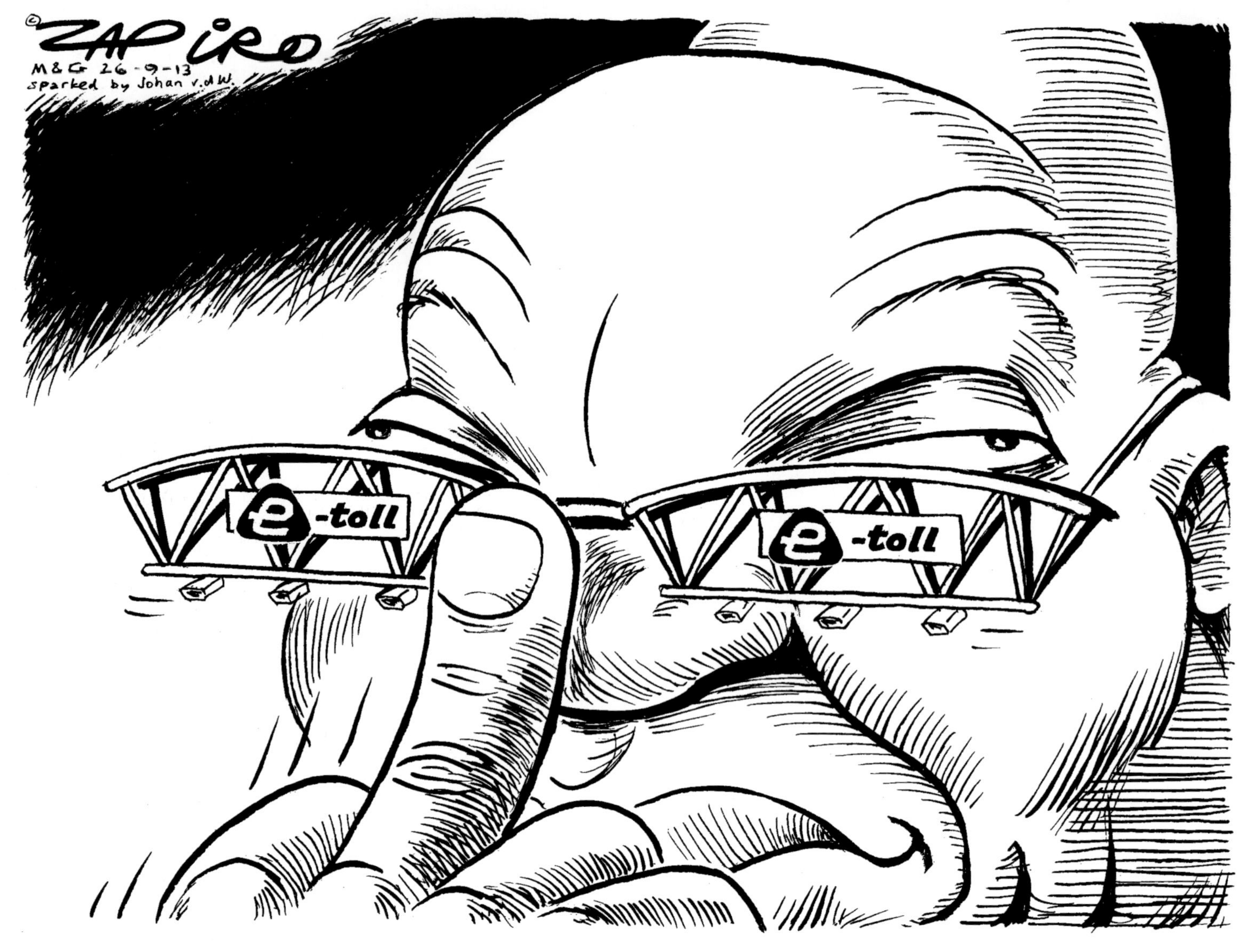

26 September 2013

… but he soon signs the equally unpopular e-tolling bill into law, which could cost his party votes in next year's election